So Cute! Baby Animals

Kittens

By Katlin Sarantou

Kittens like to play.

Kittens like to cuddle.

Kittens like to explore.

Kittens like to lick.

Kittens like to look.

Kittens like to chase.

Kittens like to swat.

Kittens like to hide.

Kittens like to climb.

Kittens like to stretch.

Kittens like to drink.

Kittens like to nap.

Word List

Kittens	look	stretch
play	chase	drink
cuddle	swat	nap
explore	hide	
lick	climb	

48 Words

Kittens like to play.
Kittens like to cuddle.
Kittens like to explore.
Kittens like to lick.
Kittens like to look.
Kittens like to chase.
Kittens like to swat.
Kittens like to hide.
Kittens like to climb.
Kittens like to stretch.
Kittens like to drink.
Kittens like to nap.

Cherry Blossom Press

Published in the United States of America by Cherry Lake Publishing Group
Ann Arbor, Michigan
www.cherrylakepublishing.com

Photo Credits: © ANUCHA PONGPATIMETH/Shutterstock.com, cover, 1; © Josep Suria/Shutterstock.com, 2; © Jane Koshchina/Shutterstock.com, 3; © FamVeld/Shutterstock.com, 4; © beton studio/Shutterstock.com, 5; © ANUCHA PONGPATIMETH/Shutterstock.com, 6; © Chendongshan/Shutterstock.com, 7; © MDavidova/Shutterstock.com, 8; © Impact Photography/Shutterstock.com, 9; © Africa Studio/Shutterstock.com, 10; © Anton Gvozdikov/Shutterstock.com, 11; © Anca Popa/Shutterstock.com, 12; © Esin Deniz/Shutterstock.com, 13; © Olhastock/Shutterstock.com, 14, back cover

Copyright © 2021 by Cherry Lake Publishing Group
All rights reserved. No part of this book may be reproduced or utilized in any form or by any means without written permission from the publisher.

Cherry Blossom Press is an imprint of Cherry Lake Publishing Group.

Library of Congress Cataloging-in-Publication Data

Names: Sarantou, Katlin, author.
Title: Kittens / by Katlin Sarantou.
Description: Ann Arbor, Michigan : Cherry Lake Publishing, [2021] | Series: So cute! baby animals | Audience: Grades K-1 | Summary: "Aww. How cute! Early readers will learn about what kittens like to do. The simple text makes it easy for children to engage in reading. Books use the Whole Language approach to literacy, a combination of sight words and repetition that builds recognition and confidence. Bold, colorful photographs correlate directly to the text to help guide readers through the book"— Provided by publisher.
Identifiers: LCCN 2020032048 (print) | LCCN 2020032049 (ebook) | ISBN 9781534179882 (paperback) | ISBN 9781534180895 (pdf) | ISBN 9781534182608 (ebook)
Subjects: LCSH: Kittens—Juvenile literature.
Classification: LCC SF445.7 .S295 2021 (print) | LCC SF445.7 (ebook) | DDC 636.8/07—dc23
LC record available at https://lccn.loc.gov/2020032048
LC ebook record available at https://lccn.loc.gov/2020032049

Printed in the United States of America
Corporate Graphics